THIS BOOK IS THE PROPERTY OF:

STATE _____

PROVINCE _____

COUNTY _____

PARISH _____

SCHOOL DISTRICT _____

OTHER _____

Book No. _____

Enter information
in space to the left
as instructed.

ISSUED TO	Year Used	CONDITION	
		ISSUED	RETURNED
_____	_____		
_____	_____		
_____	_____		
_____	_____		
_____	_____		
_____	_____		
_____	_____		
_____	_____		
_____	_____		
_____	_____		

STUDENTS to whom this textbook is issued must not write on any page
or mark any part of it in any way, consumable textbooks excepted.

1. Teachers should see that the student's name is clearly written in ink
   in the spaces above in every book issued.
2. The following terms should be used in recording the condition
   of the book: New; Good; Fair; Poor; Bad.

Growing with Mathematics
Discussion Book

Author
Calvin Irons

Contributing Authors
Sandra L. Atkins
Claire Owen

Illustrations:	Karen Ahlschläger pp. 12, 55
	Nick Buttfield p. 82
	Rae Dale pp. 14–15, 40
	John Danalis pp. 6–7, 27, 35, 41, 53, 62–63
	Ian Forss pp. 11, 50, 91
	Mary Ann Furness p. 17
	Marjorie Gardner pp. 17, 43
	Matt O'Neill pp. 2–3, 8–9
	Peter Shaw pp. 22, 73, 83, 89
	Craig Smith p. 80
	Chantal Stewart p. 18
	Gaston Vanzet pp. 24, 57, 60, 64, 87, 94–95
Photography:	David Johns

Acknowledgments: The authors would like to thank all the mathematics educators, teachers, and students who participated in the development of this book.
Special thanks go to: Honi Bamberger, Elisa Torstensson, Wendy Foreman, Mari Muri, Kelly Anderson, and Shelley Farrar-Coleman; to Joan Vinall, Jaime Norris, and Grade 2 students from Alice D. Contreras Elementary School, Fort Worth ISD for piloting the pages; to Pauline Taylor, Trish Maloney, Maria Kristianson, Rieky Wielens, Susie Colla, and Grade 1 and 2 students at St. Robert's Elementary School for contributing artwork; Meg Carroll, Alice Curran, Samuel Everett, Elise Kavpinski, and Georgette Paatsch for the illustrations on pages 46, 65, and 81; Matthew Balshaw, Julia-Rose Tanton, Ike Ogbonnaya, Daniel Eddy, Sharelle Chan (Ruby), and Sarah Khan for their participation in the photography sessions.

www.WrightGroup.com

Wright Group

Copyright © 2004 by Wright Group/McGraw-Hill.

Printed in the United States of America.

Send all inquiries to:
Wright Group/McGraw-Hill
P.O. Box 812960
Chicago, IL 60681

ISBN 0-322-06972-6

2 3 4 5 6 7 8 9 MAL 09 08 07 06 05 04

The **McGraw·Hill** Companies

CONTENTS

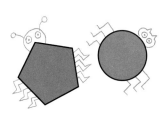

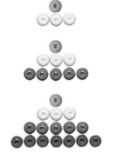

TOPIC 5: Adding and Subtracting 2-Digit Numbers

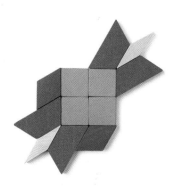

TOPIC 6: Working with Money, Time, and Data

TOPIC 7: More Measurement and Geometry

TOPIC 8: Place Value: Numbers to 1,000

TOPIC 9: More Addition and Subtraction of Two-Digit Numbers

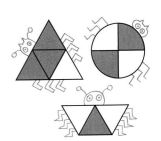

TOPIC 10: Fractions, Probability, and Time

TOPIC 11: Multiplication and Division Concepts

TOPIC 12: Working with Numbers to 1,000

What can you count?
What numbers can you see?

Just Juice

8 Cool Combinations

95¢   80¢   65¢

8th Street

Beach
75 yards

Fun Park
3 miles

1. Which of these amounts are worth more than a quarter?

2. Give another way to show each amount.

3. Choose two purses. Which amount is greater?

1. Count the wheels, the creatures, and the stars.
(Count by 2s, 5s, and 10s.)

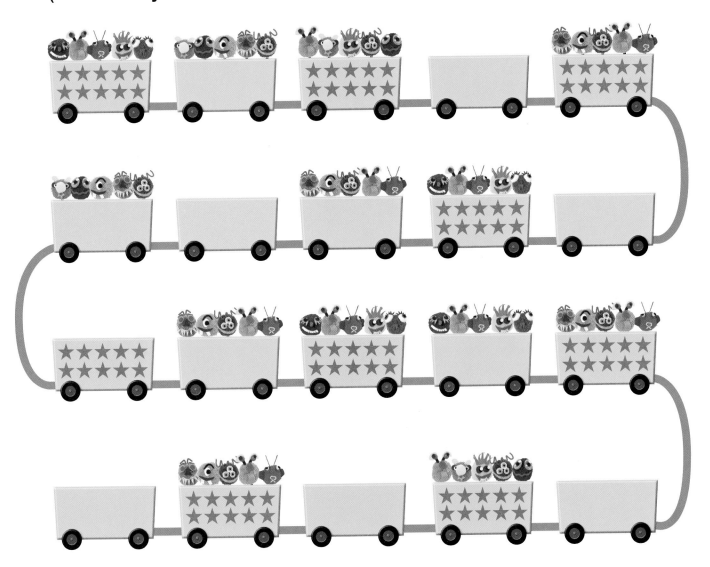

2. Count by 5s to find how many creatures could ride:

| in the empty cars | on the whole "train" |

3. How many  would you draw to show:

| 50 wheels? | 50 creatures? | 50 stars? |

1. How do you think the Super Sorter works?

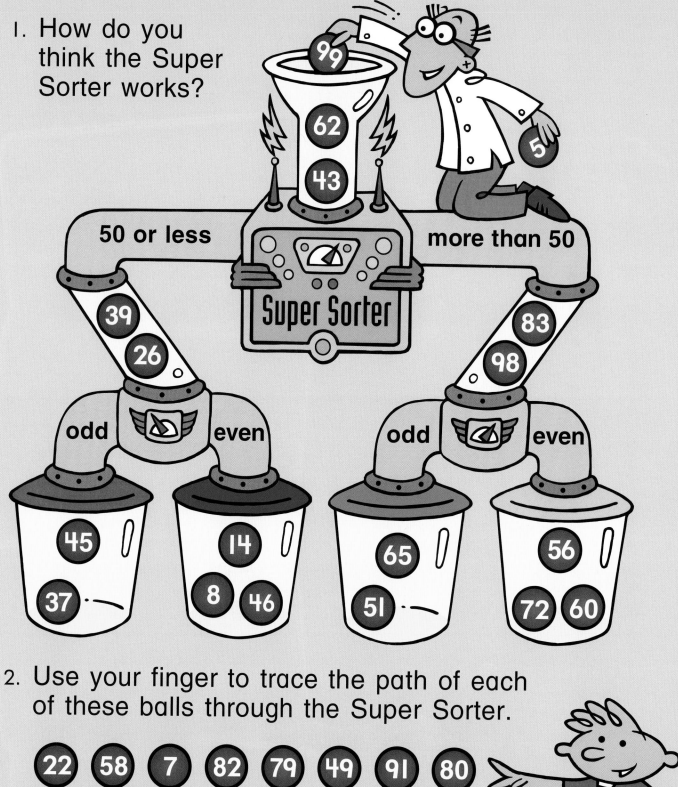

50 or less

more than 50

Super Sorter

odd   even

odd   even

2. Use your finger to trace the path of each of these balls through the Super Sorter.

22 58 7 82 79 49 91 80

3. Which bins would hold numbers you say when you count:

by 2s?   by 10s?   by 5s?

1. Look at each clock. Say the time.
   What do **you** do at that time?

Pirate Pete's Day

2. Pick 2 of the clocks.
   Figure out the difference in time.

Make up addition stories.
Write the number facts.

SCOREBOARD

INNING	1	2	3	4	5	6	7	8	9
RED	0	1	4	0					
BLUE	3	1	2						

1. Choose one pizza and one drink.
   Count on to find the total cost.
   Write two addition facts.

Cheese
Medium $4
Large $6

Pepperoni
Medium $5
Large $7

Vegetarian
Medium $6
Large $8

Special
Medium $7
Large $9

Regular $1

Large $2

Giant $3

2. Find all possible solutions for these problems.

Joe bought one pizza and a drink. He spent $8. What did he buy?

Chantelle spent $15 on two pizzas and a drink. What did she buy?

1. How did Katy Kangaroo use a "double" to figure out these addition facts?

4 + 5 = ____

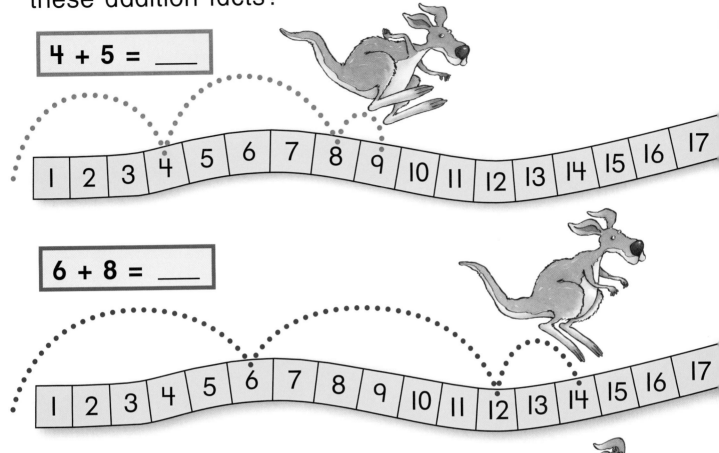

6 + 8 = ____

7 + 8 = ____

2. How would Katy figure out these "near doubles"?

8 + 9 = ____

6 + 7 = ____

7 + 9 = ____

5 + 7 = ____

9 + 7 = ____

6 + 5 = ____

12 + 13 = ____

10 + 11 = ____

11 + 13 = ____

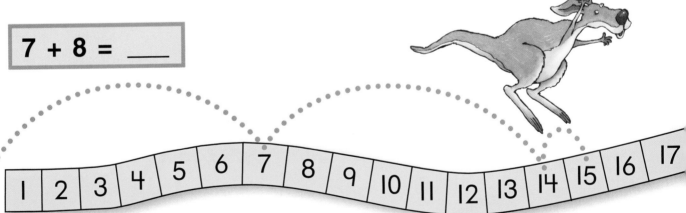

Make up two subtraction problems for each picture.
(You could cover one group of animals
at a time to help.)
Write the subtraction facts.

1. How much does each toy cost?

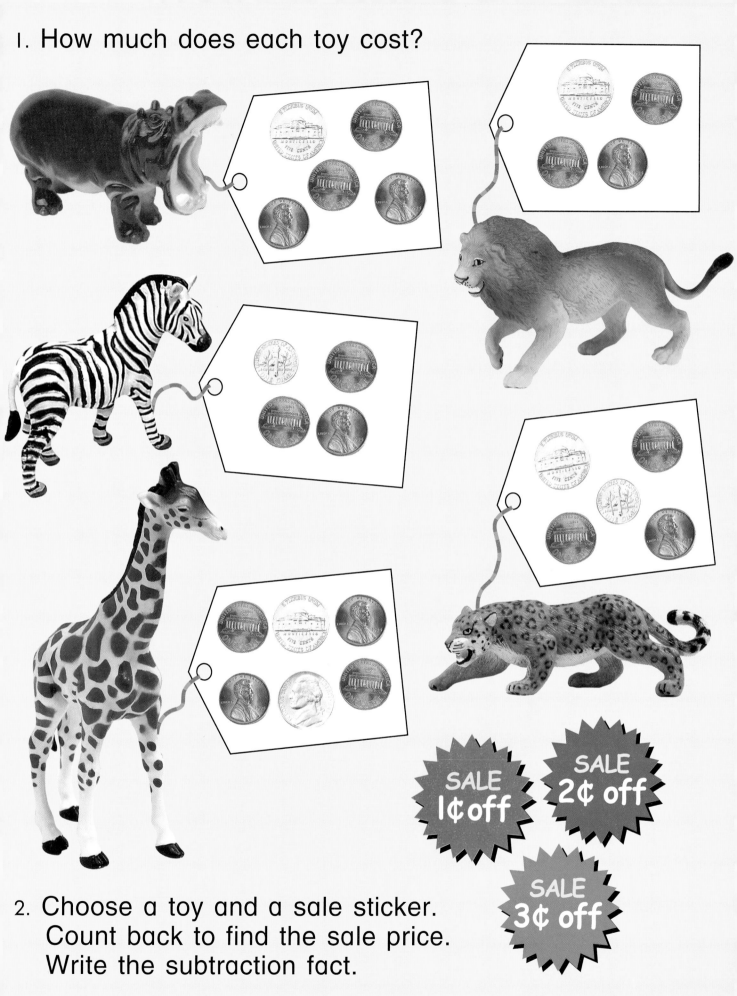

2. Choose a toy and a sale sticker.
Count back to find the sale price.
Write the subtraction fact.

SALE
1¢ off

SALE
2¢ off

SALE
3¢ off

Make up and solve story problems.
Write a number sentence for each.

Giant
Pumpkins
$4

Small
Pumpkins
$2

1. How many children voted for their favorite sport?

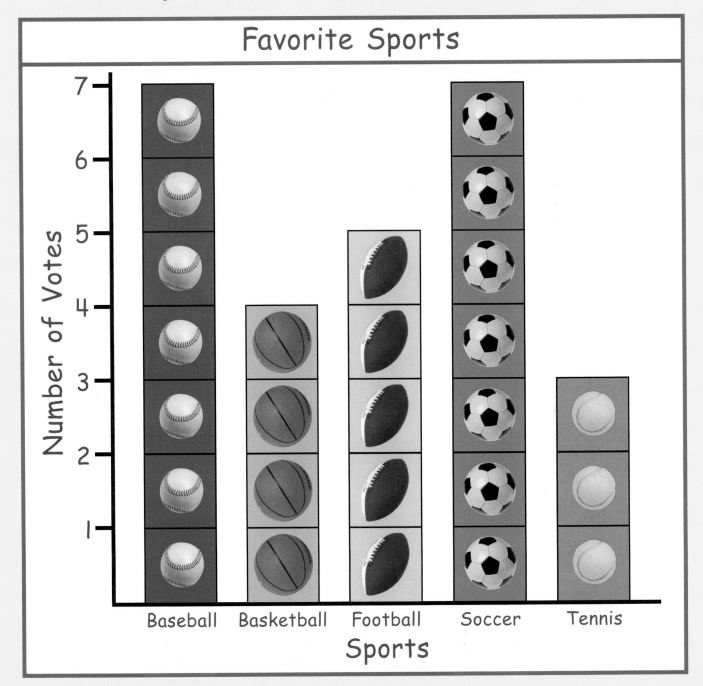

Favorite Sports

2. Pick two of the sports and solve this problem.

> How many more people voted
> for _____ than for _____ ?

3. Make up and solve other problems about the data.

Find something in the pictures you could measure. Which of these tools would you use?

 or or

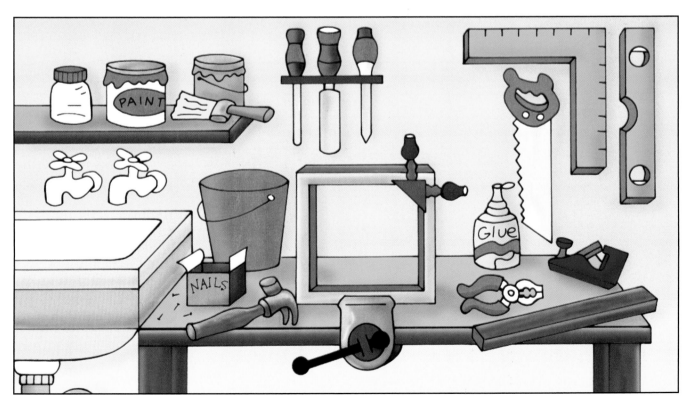

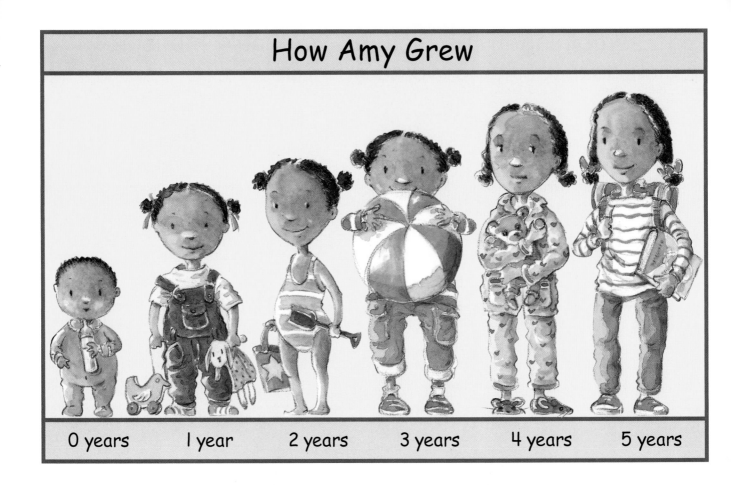

How Amy Grew

| 0 years | 1 year | 2 years | 3 years | 4 years | 5 years |

1. How tall was Amy when she was 3 years old?

2. How old was Amy when she was:

   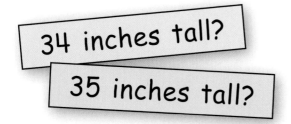
   34 inches tall?

   35 inches tall?

3. How tall do you think Amy will be when she is 6 years old?

4. How many inches did Amy grow each year?

5. How many years did it take Amy to double her birth height?

Age (years)	Height (inches)
0	21
1	30
2	34
3	37
4	40
5	42

1. What are the children measuring with one-inch tiles?

2. Which of the tile "trains" are longer than one foot?

3. Pick 2 tile trains and find the **difference** in length. Now find the **total** length. Is it:

less than 1 foot?

equal to 1 foot?

between 1 foot and 2 feet?

more than 2 feet?

1. How many one-centimeter cubes were joined together to make this "train"?

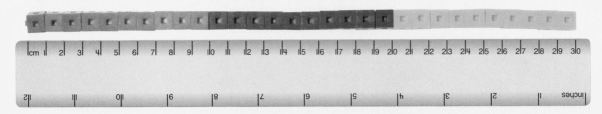

2. Estimate each of the lengths below in centimeters. Then count the cubes to check.

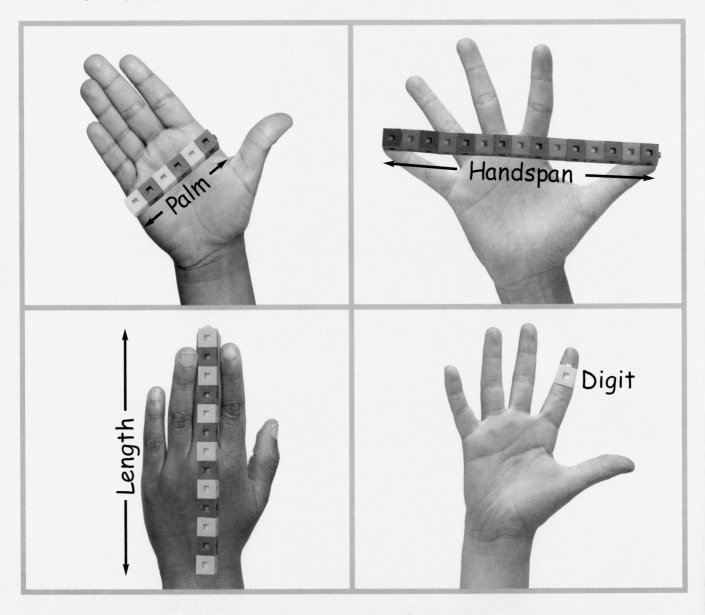

Palm

Handspan

Length

Digit

3. How much longer or shorter than 10 cm is each of the lengths above?
How much shorter than 30 cm is each length?

1. Whose giant step was closest to 1 meter? How did you decide?

2. How much less than 1 meter is each of the giant steps?

3. How much less than 1 meter are these lengths?

Our Giant Steps

Julia	75 cm
Daniel	90 cm
Ike	85 cm
Sarah	93 cm
Matthew	89 cm
Sharelle	82 cm

← 25 cm →

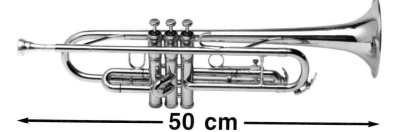

← 50 cm →

← 30 cm →

1. What shapes can you find in this picture?

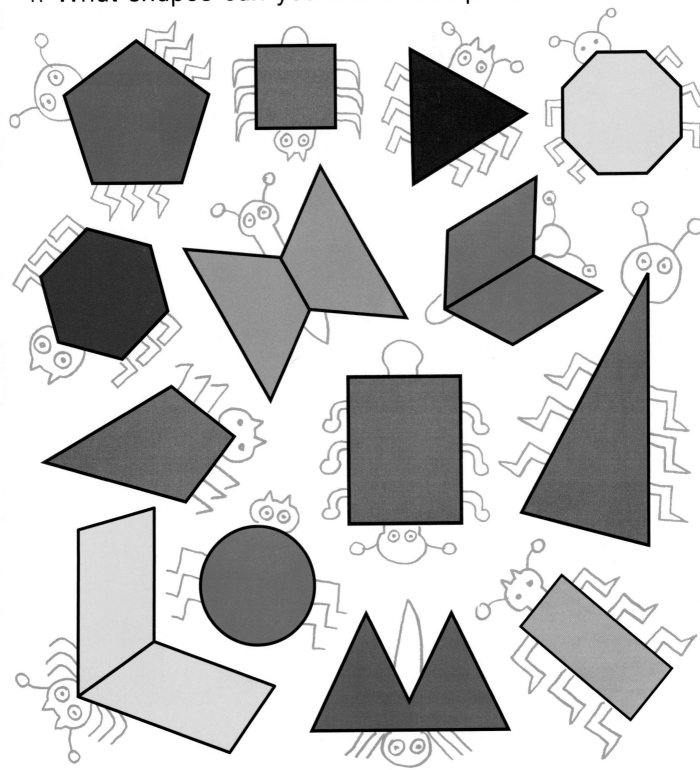

2. Find lines in the shapes that are:

parallel   not parallel   horizontal   vertical

1. What shapes did each person make?

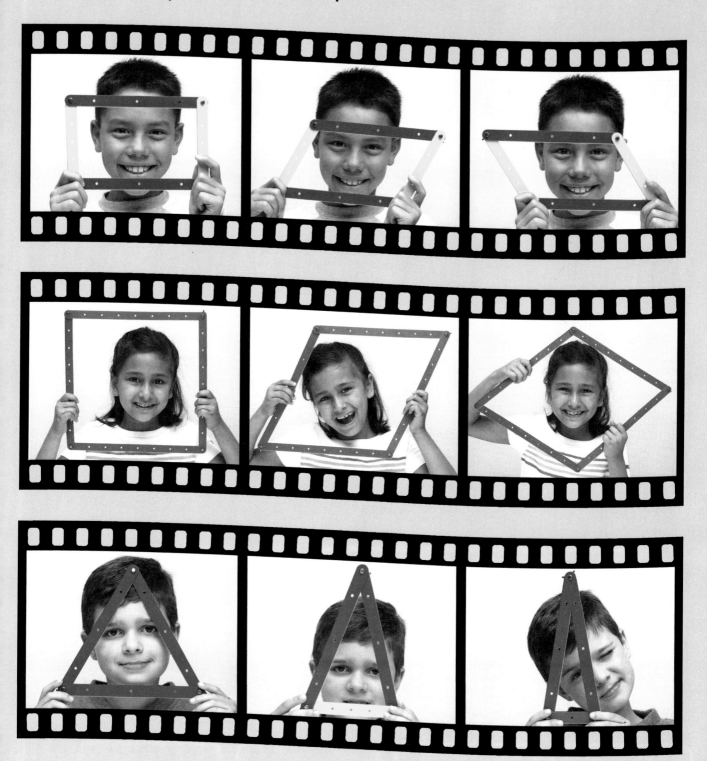

2. How are each person's 3 shapes alike?
   How are they different?

3. How did each person change the first shape
   to make the other two shapes?

1. What 3-D shapes can you find in the picture?
   What 2-D shapes can you see?

2. Which of the 3-D shapes have:

only flat faces? | a curved surface?

at least one face that is a triangle?

Pick a clue. Find a 3-D shape to match.
How does it match?
Do any of the other shapes also match?

I have an
even number of
flat faces.

I have no edges,
vertices, or faces.

I have 5 vertices.

I have more than
5 vertices.

I have an
odd number of
flat faces.

I have 12 edges.

I have no edges.

I have more than
10 vertices.

1. Look at each peg-board pattern.
   How does the pattern **grow**?

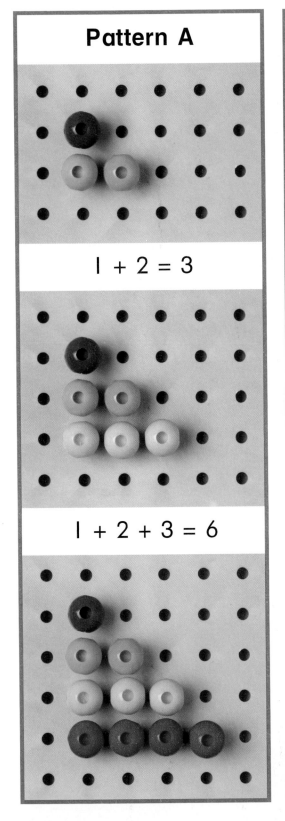

Pattern A

1 + 2 = 3

1 + 2 + 3 = 6

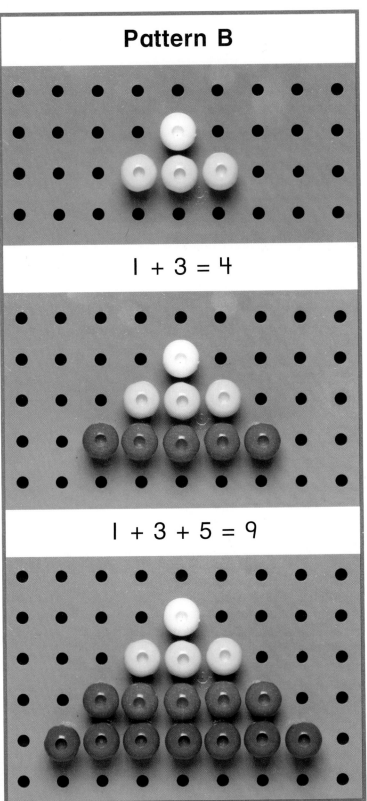

Pattern B

1 + 3 = 4

1 + 3 + 5 = 9

2. Write the next 2 addition sentences for each pattern.

1. What happened when these tens and ones blocks went through the Trade-a-Ten machine?

Before   Trade-a-Ten   After

2. What blocks will you see **after** these blocks go through the Trade-a-Ten machine?

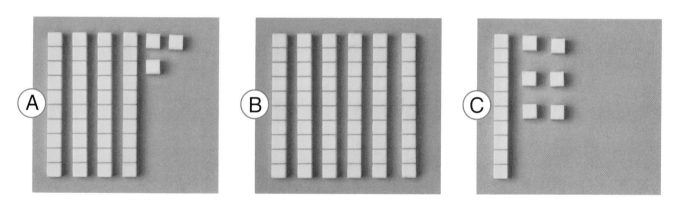

A   B   C

3. What would you have seen **before** these blocks went through the machine?

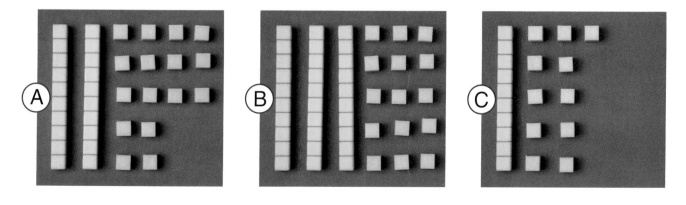

A   B   C

In how many ways can you find **one hundred**?

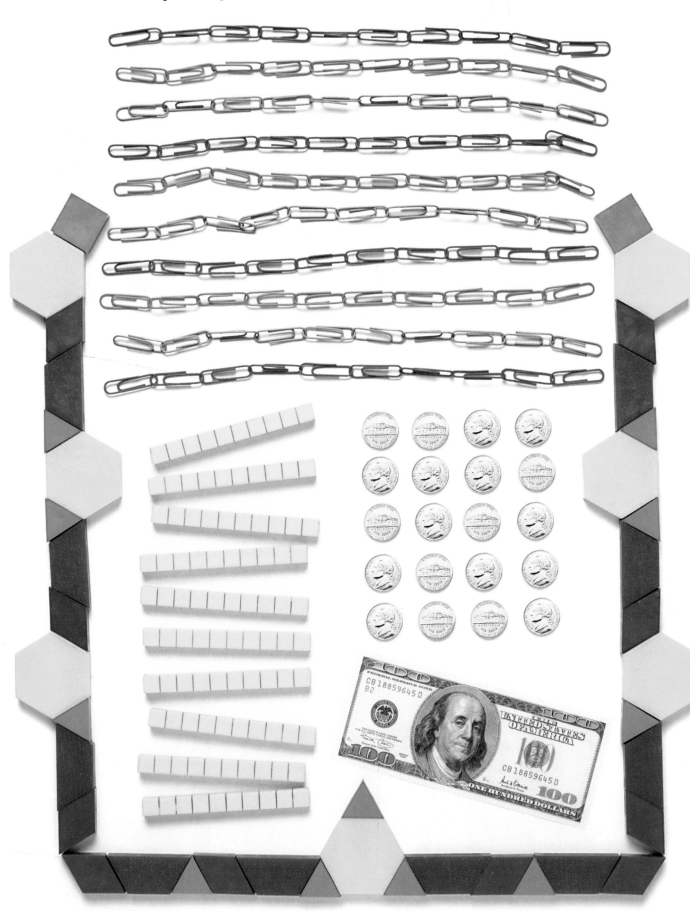

1. How many **beans** are on the bean **boat**?

2. How many **boats** were used to make this **raft**? How many **beans** are on the **raft**?

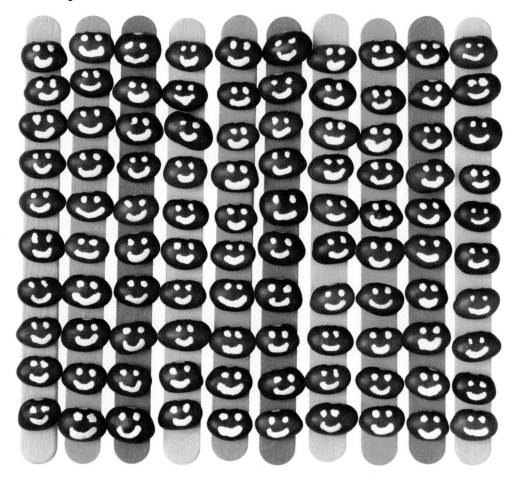

3. How many **hundreds**, **tens**, and **ones** does each of these bean pictures show?

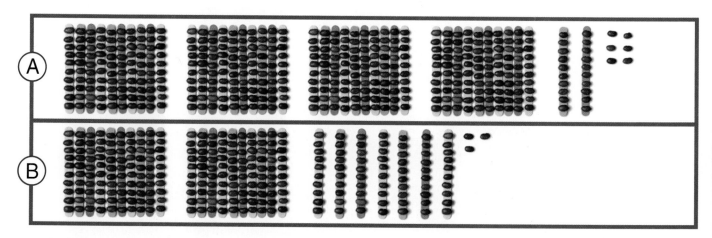

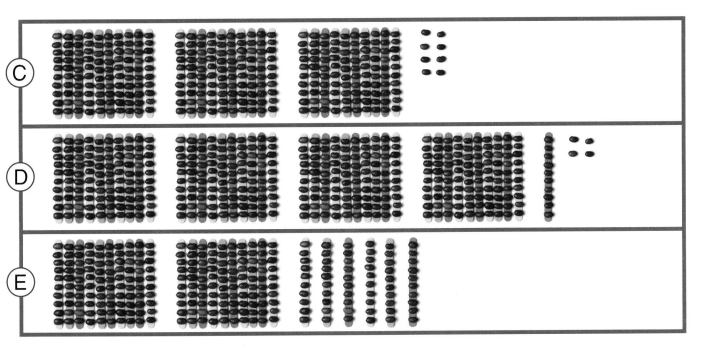

4. Read this open expander.
   Which of the bean pictures does it describe?

Now read the closed expander.
How does it help you say the number of beans?

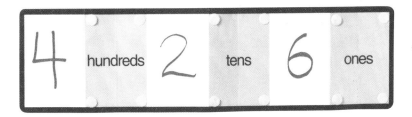

5. What would you write on the open expander for
   each of the other bean pictures?
   How would you say the number?

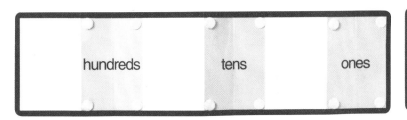 

1. Choose two pictures at a time.
   Which number is **greater**?
   How did you decide?

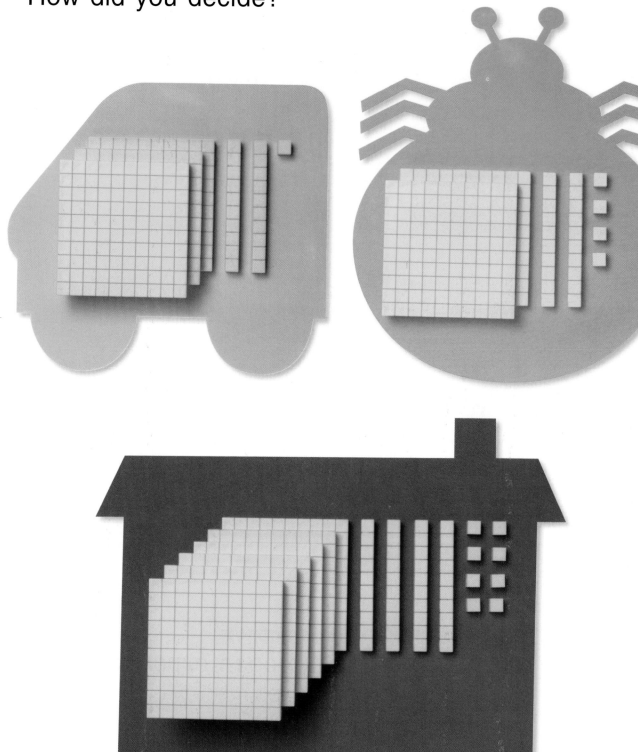

2. Choose three pictures at a time.
   Write the numbers in order.

3. For each of the pictures, give the number that is:

100 more   10 more   1 more
100 less   10 less   1 less

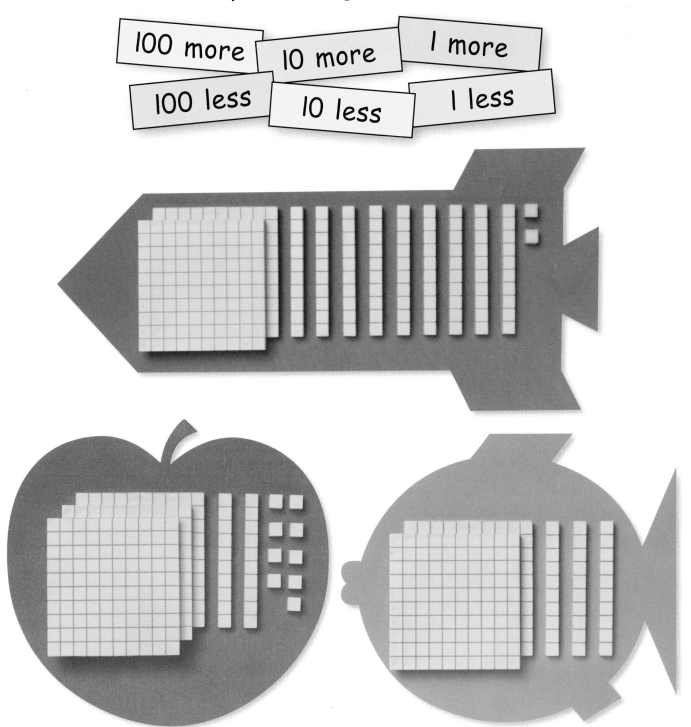

4. How would you change each picture to show:

the next ten?   the previous ten?
the next hundred?   the previous hundred?

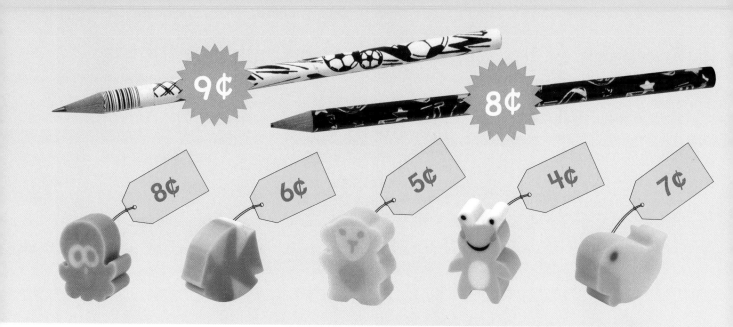

1. Renata bought the  and the .
   She paid with a dime and some pennies.
   What do these addition sentences show?

   5¢   9¢

   | 9 + 5 = ___ |

   | 10 + 4 = ___ |

   How much did Renata spend?

2. Choose a pencil and an eraser.
   How would you pay with a dime and pennies?
   Write addition sentences to show the total cost.

3. Find the missing numbers.
   What patterns do you see?

   | 10 + 5 = ___ |
   | 9 + 6 = ___ |
   | 8 + 7 = ___ |

   | 10 + ___ = 13 |
   | 9 + ___ = 13 |
   | 8 + ___ = 13 |

   | 10 + 15 = ___ |
   | 9 + 16 = ___ |
   | 8 + 17 = ___ |

1. Give the OUT number for each of these IN numbers.

| 2 | 4 | 6 | 15 | 18 | 19 |

2. Give the IN number for each of these OUT numbers.

| 12 | 16 | 18 | 20 | 23 | 25 |

Did you add or subtract to find the IN numbers?

3. Find the missing numbers.

IN	8	13			21	
OUT			19	29		21

1. How would you figure out the total cost of these?

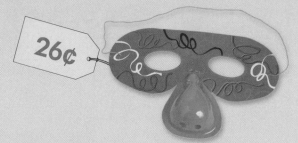 26¢

 9¢

2. How did these children show their thinking?

Bianca

$26 + 9$

Trade 10 □
for 1 ▭
$30 + 5 = 35$

Tan

Use a 100 chart.
Start at 26.
Jump 10 ↓.
Jump back 1 ←.

$26 + 10 - 1 = 35$

Victor

Start at 26.
Jump 4 to 30.
Then jump
5 more.

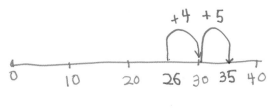

$26 + 4 + 5 = 35$

Shyann

I know 9 + 6.
Then I used a
number pattern.

$9 + 6 = 15$
$9 + 16 = 25$
$9 + 26 = 35$

1. Daniel is going to throw his second beanbag.
   What totals could he get?

2. Use numbers from the target to make these
   sentences true.

25 = ___ + ___	30 = ___ + ___
40 = ___ + ___	50 = ___ + ___
60 = ___ + ___	75 = ___ + ___
85 = ___ + ___	90 = ___ + ___

Solve each problem.
Draw pictures or write number sentences
to show your thinking.

Wendy bought
2 dinosaurs. She
spent 40 cents.
Which dinosaurs did
she buy?

Curtis has 40 cents.
Pick 2 dinosaurs he
can buy. What is
the total cost?

Pick 2 dinosaurs that
cost about 50 cents
in all. What is the
exact cost?

Rosa has 60 cents.
How could she spend
all of her money?

1. How would you figure out the amount left?

2. How did these children figure out the amount left?

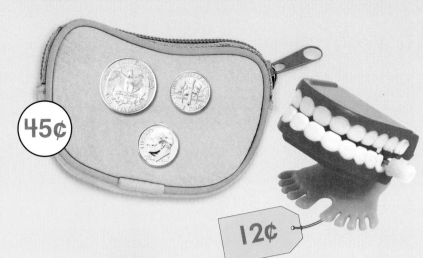

45¢

12¢

Bianca

40 - 10 = 30
5 - 2 = 3
45 - 12 = 33

Tan

Use a 100 chart.
Start at 45.
Jump back 10 ↑.
Jump back 2 ←.

1	2	3	4	5	6	7	8	9	10
11	12	13	14	15	16	17	18	19	20
21	22	23	24	25	26	27	28	29	30
31	32	33	34	35	36	37	38	39	40
41	42	43	44	45	46	47	48	49	50

45 - 10 - 2 = 33

Victor

Start at 45.
Jump back by 5s.
Jump back 2 more.

45 - 5 = 40   40 - 5 = 35
35 - 2 = 33

Shyann

Take away one dime.
Trade the other dime then take 2 pennies.

25 ⊗ ⊗ ① ① ⑤ ① ①

45 - 10 - 2 = 33

1. What steps do you think Ben used to make the "graph" below?

2. Which of Ben's bean plants are **taller** than 50 cm? How much taller are they?

Height of Ben's Bean Plants

68cm 62cm 36 cm 45cm 59 cm 54cm

A B C D E F

3. Which of Ben's plants are **shorter** than 50 cm? How much shorter are they?

4. Find pairs of plants with a height difference that is **less** than 10 cm. What are those differences?

1. Dan has 41 cents. He wants to buy the 29¢ penguin. Why do you think he put his coins through the Trade-a-Ten machine?
How much will Dan have left?

Before   **After**

2. Pick one of these amounts and one thing to buy. Would you need to "trade a ten"?
How much would you have left?

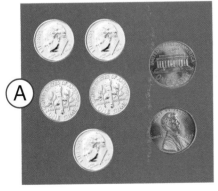
(A)

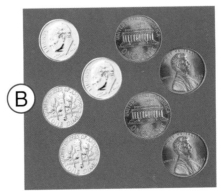
(B)

(C)

Pick a story problem.
Will you add or subtract to solve it?
Now figure out the answer. Show your thinking.

Meghan

I bought a muffin and it cost 25 cents.
I bought a drink and it cost 23¢.
How much did I spend in all?

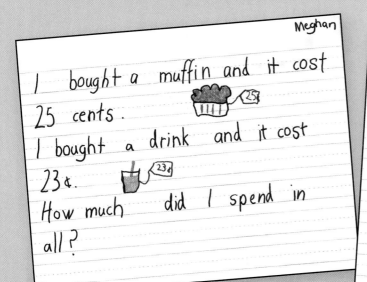

Zackary

One day a boy had 85¢. He went to the mall and he bought a toy robot that cost 60¢. How much did he have left?

Tayla

I had $48. I worked in the yard so Dad gave me $13. How much money do I have now?

$13 $48

Dino

I looked in my Piggy bank and I had 39 cents. Then Mom put some more money in and then I had 54 cents. How much did Mom give me?

Miguel

I saw a toy plane. It was 54 cents. I saw a toy car and it was 23 cents. How much more was the plane?

54¢   23¢

Wendy

My friend Amy had 50 cents. She bought a hair clip and then she had 19 cents left. How much was the hair clip?

Pick two piggy banks. Is the total amount:

- more than one dollar?
- less than one dollar?
- equal to one dollar?

1. How would you figure out the cost of 12 balloons?

BALLOONS
3 for 20¢

HATS
2 for 15¢

WHISTLES
4 for 30¢

2. How did these children show their thinking?

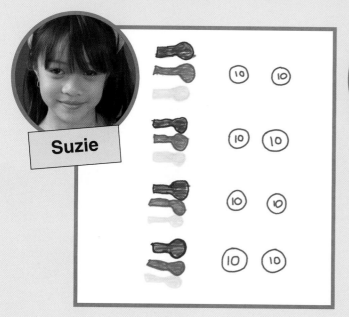

Suzie

Jordan

Number	Cost
3 balloons	20¢
6 balloons	40¢
9 balloons	60¢
12 balloons	80¢

3. Solve these problems. Explain your thinking.

Rosa bought
12 whistles. How
much did they cost?

Cesar bought
10 hats. How
much did he spend?

Natalie spent 60¢ on
whistles. How many
whistles did she buy?

Paul spent 60¢
on hats. How many
hats did he buy?

1. About how long would each of these bedtime activities take?
How did you decide what measurement **units** to use in your answers?

2. List some activities that take:

about one second

about one minute

about one hour

about one day

1. **For each of these weekend activities, read the two clocks. How long did the activity take?**

Start I watched cartoons. **Stop** 9:00

I played soccer. 11:30

I had lunch with Grandma. 12:30

I played with my friend. 3:00

2. **Pick any two of the clocks. Find the time difference.**

1. Ms. Owen's class surveyed all of the first-graders and second-graders. What steps do you think the class used to collect and display the data?

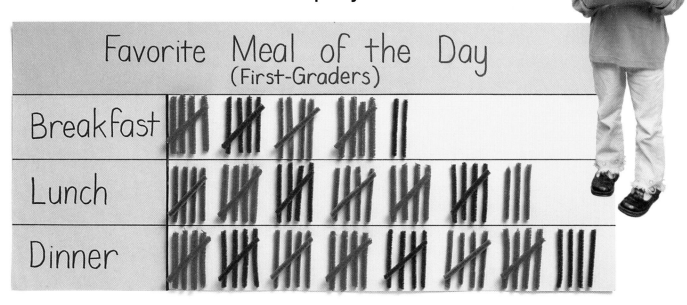

Favorite Meal of the Day
(First-Graders)

Breakfast	
Lunch	
Dinner	

Favorite Meal of the Day
(Second-Graders)

= 5 votes

Breakfast	
Lunch	
Dinner	

2. How many children at each grade level chose:

breakfast? lunch? dinner?

3. How many **more** children at each grade level voted for dinner than for breakfast?

1. What steps did Ms. Owen's class use to make this graph?

2. What does each X on the graph represent? How many children helped make the graph?

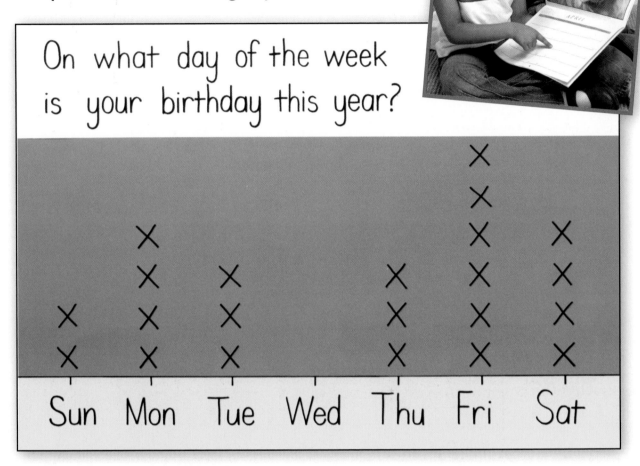

On what day of the week is your birthday this year?

| Sun | Mon | Tue | Wed | Thu | Fri | Sat |

3. How many children have their birthday this year:

on a Monday? on a Thursday? on the weekend?

4. How many **more** people have their birthday this year on **Friday** than on:

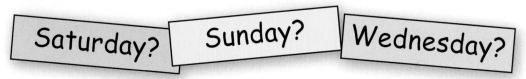

Saturday? Sunday? Wednesday?

1. How many lines of symmetry can you find
   in each of these designs?

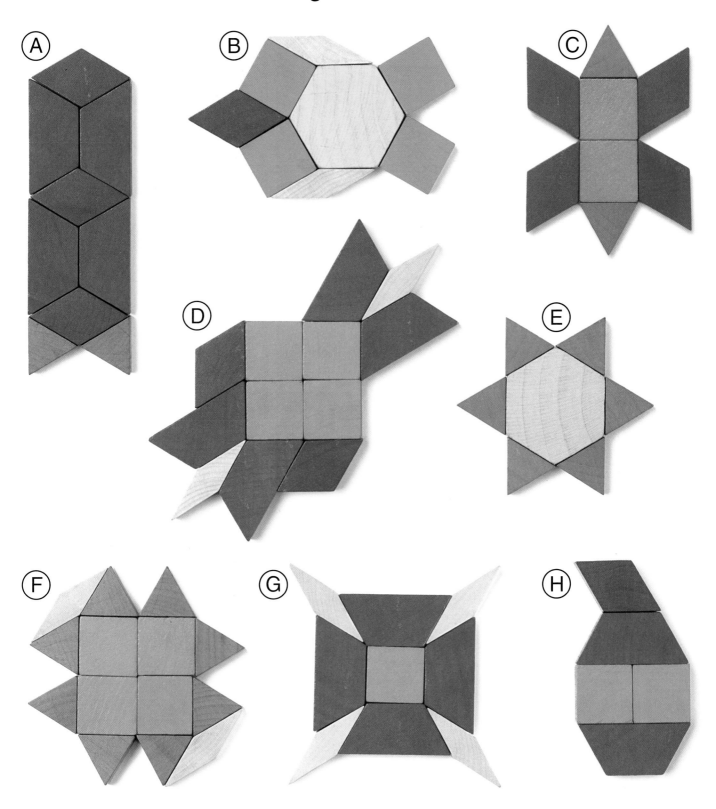

Ⓐ   Ⓑ   Ⓒ

Ⓓ   Ⓔ

Ⓕ   Ⓖ   Ⓗ

2. Which blocks could you take away, so that **every
   design** has exactly 2 lines of symmetry?

1. What shapes did the mice make from this rectangle?

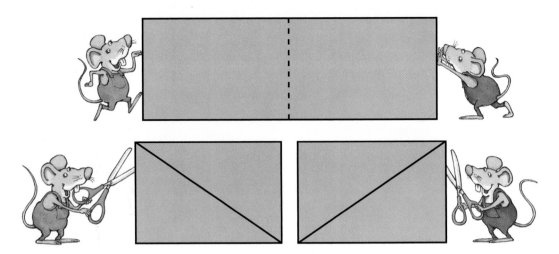

2. Describe the shapes that the mice made with the triangles.

   Where can you see:
   • square corners?
   • parallel lines?

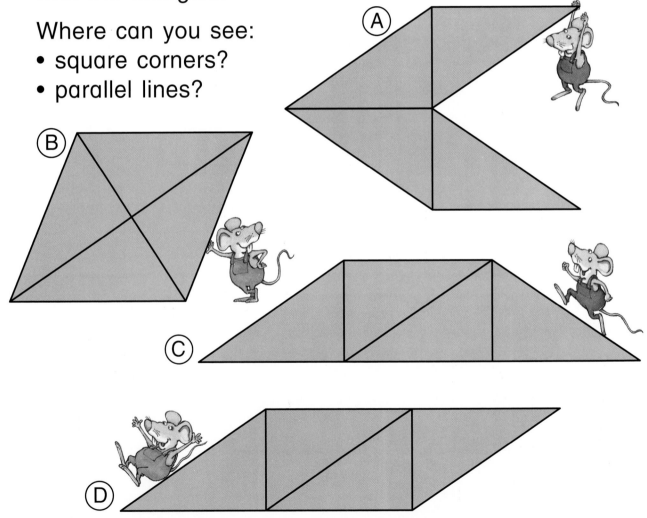

3. What other shapes could the mice make with all 4 triangles?

1. Pick a **red** shape. How could you **flip**, **turn**, or **slide** it so that it covers another red shape in the same design?

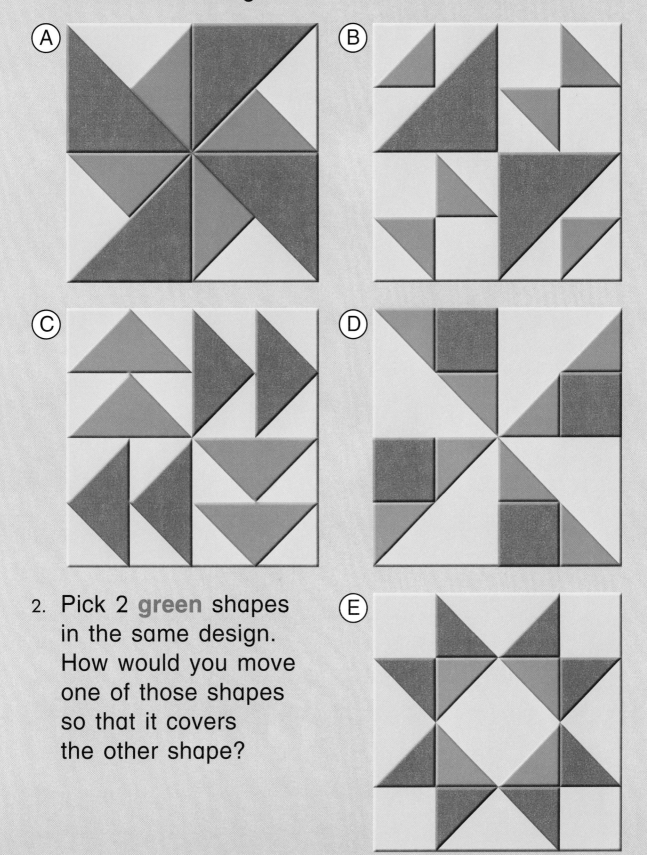

2. Pick 2 **green** shapes in the same design. How would you move one of those shapes so that it covers the other shape?

Which of the 2 photographs did each child take? Where was the camera when the other photograph was taken?

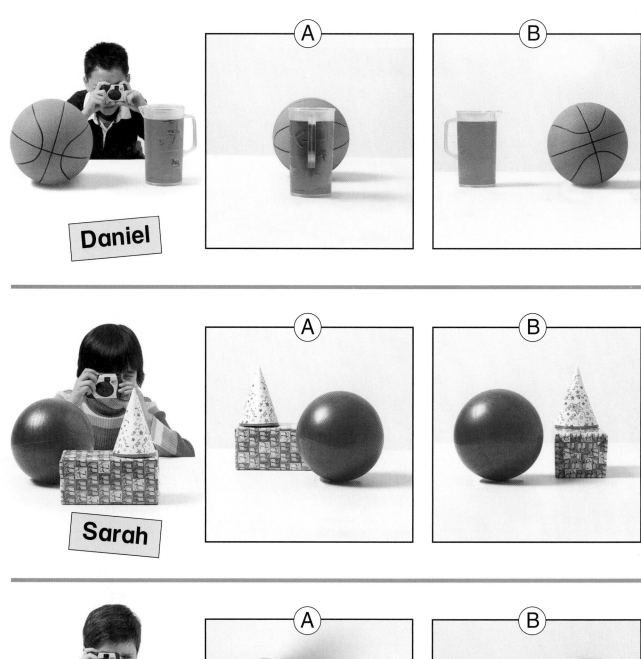

Daniel

A

B

Sarah

A

B

Matthew

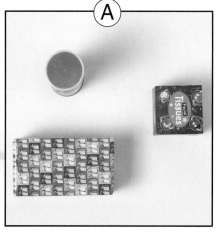

A

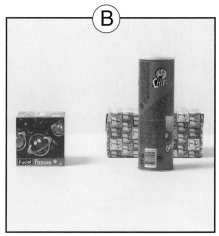

B

B) Forward 3.
Turn right.
Forward 2.
Turn left.
Forward 3.
Turn left.
Forward 4.

1. Do both sets of directions lead Pirate Pete to the treasure (✗)?

2. Give directions for another path that Pete could follow to get to the treasure.

3. Now give directions from the treasure to the boat.

1. What steps do you think Daniel used to put **1 pound** of food into each of the jars below?

2. Would **1 cup** of **corn** and **1 cup** of **oats** weigh the same amount? How do you know?

3. Which of these cups of food is:

heaviest?

lightest?

in between?

4. Pick one of the jars above. Estimate how much of that food would balance **1 cup** of **rice**.

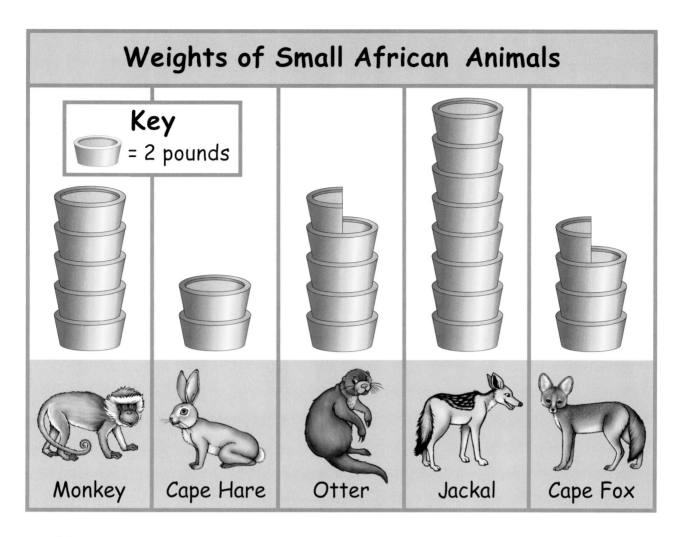

Weights of Small African Animals

Key
= 2 pounds

Monkey | Cape Hare | Otter | Jackal | Cape Fox

1. How much does each animal on the graph weigh? Which animal is the heaviest?

2. Pick 2 animals on the graph. Copy and complete this sentence.

> The _____ weighs _____ pounds more than the _____ .

3. How would you show these weights on the graph?

20 pounds

Anteater

2 pounds

Meerkat

1 pound

Tortoise

15 pounds

Wildcat

1. What did Matthew and Ruby find out about:

pints and cups?

quarts and cups?

quarts and pints?

1 cup   1 pint   1 quart

2. Answer each of these questions in at least 2 ways.

Pick **one** container. How much does it hold?

Pick **two** containers. How much do they hold in all?

Pick **two** containers. How much more does the larger container hold?

4 cups — A

8 cups — B

2 cups — C

6 cups — D

3 cups — E

Glass (1 cup) 10¢
Bottle (2 cups) 15¢
Pitcher (4 cups) 25¢

1. Ellie Elephant bought:

How many **cups** of lemonade did Ellie buy altogether?
How many **pints** is that?
How many **quarts**?

How much did Ellie pay for the lemonade?

2. Find all possible answers for these problems.

Ⓐ How much lemonade could you buy for exactly 50 cents?

Ⓑ How much would it cost to buy 1 quart of lemonade?

3. How many glasses, bottles, and/or pitchers of lemonade did each of these elephants buy?

I bought 3 pints of lemonade for 55 cents.

I bought 5 cups of lemonade for 35 cents.

Elva

Edwin

1. **Look at these pictures. What do you notice?**

2. **Pick a picture. What number does it show? How would each of the other children show that number?**

1. What number does each block picture show?

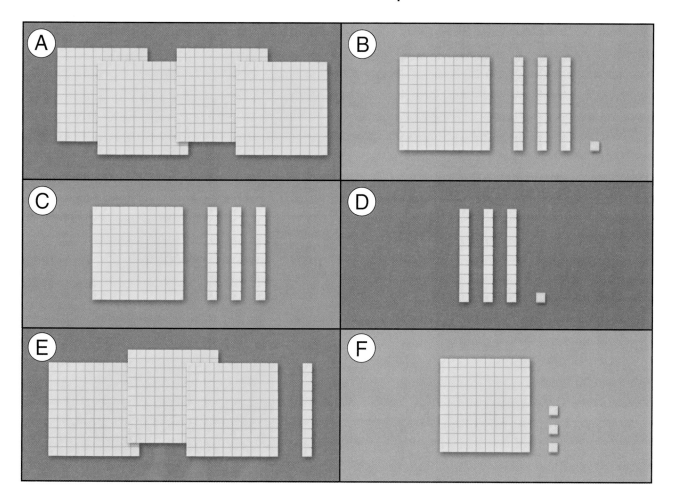

2. For each of Billy's clues, find the pictures above that match.

3. Write the number(s) for the pictures that match:

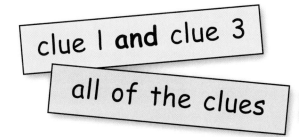

clue 1 **and** clue 3

all of the clues

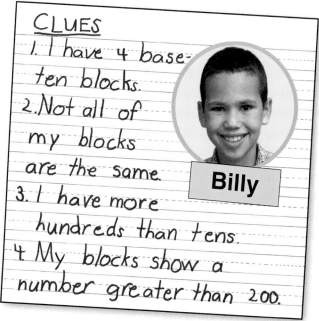

CLUES
1. I have 4 base-ten blocks.
2. Not all of my blocks are the same.
3. I have more hundreds than tens.
4. My blocks show a number greater than 200.

Billy

4. Use blocks to show other three-digit numbers that match all of Billy's clues. Write each number.

Pick any 2 of the prices. Which of those prices is **greater**? How did you decide?

Spiral Slide $525

Spring Seesaw $559

Loops Challenge $719

S-Bars $759

Double Slide $650

Rings Challenge $655

Spiral Climber $699

Now copy and complete both of these sentences for the prices you picked.

____ is less than ____.
____ < ____.

1. What number does each row of blocks show?

Hundreds	Tens	Ones
(A)		
(B)		
(C)		

2. Pick one of the numbers above and one of the labels on this spinner. What would the new number be? What part of the number would change?

Spinner labels: 10 more, 1 more, 1 less, 10 less, 100 less, 100 more

3. Pick a number below. Write the numbers that are:
100 more, 100 less, 10 more, 10 less, 1 more, 1 less.

825   481   450   319

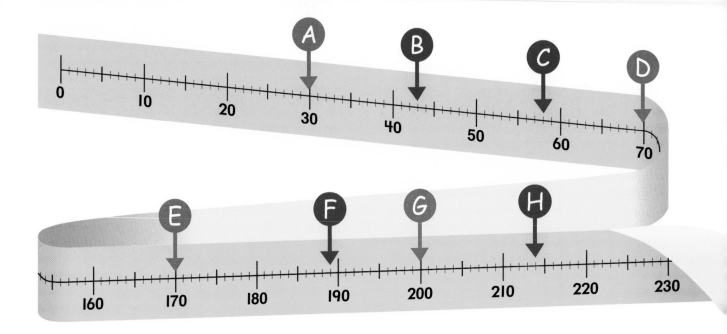

1. Pick a **red** arrow on this page. Count **on** by tens from that number to the end of the number line.

2. Pick a **red** arrow on page 63. Count **back** by tens from that number.

3. Pick any 2 **red** arrows. Count by tens from one arrow to the other. How many "jumps" of 10 did you make? How did you figure it out?

4. Pick a **blue** arrow. Predict the last number you will say if you count **on** by tens along the number line. Count on by tens to check your prediction.

5. Pick a **blue** arrow.
   Which two "tens" is it between?
   Which of those "tens" is nearer?

6. Pick one of the arrows
   from **I** to **P** .
   Which two "hundreds" is it between?
   Which of those "hundreds" is nearer?
   How did you decide?

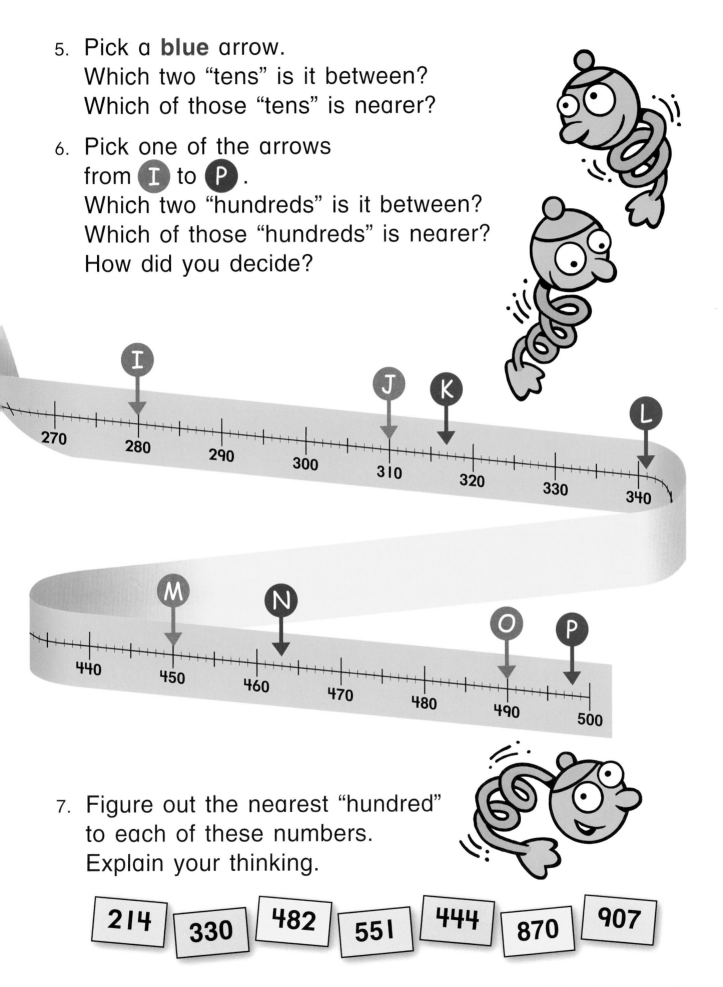

7. Figure out the nearest "hundred"
   to each of these numbers.
   Explain your thinking.

214   330   482   551   444   870   907

OUTER SPACE PARK

Rocket Ride **15¢**   Space Race **25¢**   Lunar Launch **45¢**

Splashdown! **35¢**   Jumpin' Jupiter **20¢**   Big Dipper **30¢**

Solve each problem. Write the addition sentence.

(A) I'm going on the 3 rides that cost the least. How much money do I need?

(B) I'm going on the Rocket Ride 3 times! How much will that cost?

(C) I'm going to spend 50 cents on 3 rides. Which rides are they?

(D) I have 90 cents. Do I have enough money to go on 4 different rides?

(E) I have $1 and I'm going to spend it all! Which 3 rides can I go on?

1. Solve each of the story problems.
   Show your thinking.

A Audrey

I spent some money at the school store. I bought a pen that cost 37¢ and I bought a notepad. It was 41¢. How much money did I spend?

B Jimmy

Some second-graders went to the zoo. 52 children rode the school bus and 24 children rode the mini bus. How many children went to the zoo?

C Nathaniel

I have 36 basketball cards. My sister has 25 cards. She says she will give her cards to me. How many cards will I have then?

D Kara

My Dad is 42 years old. My Grandad is 28 years older than Dad. How old is Grandad?

2. Pick two of the numbers on the spinner.
   Write and illustrate an addition story problem that uses those two numbers.

1. How would you figure out the total cost of the watches?

2. How did Suzie find the total cost?

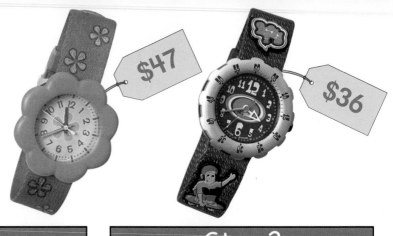

$47

$36

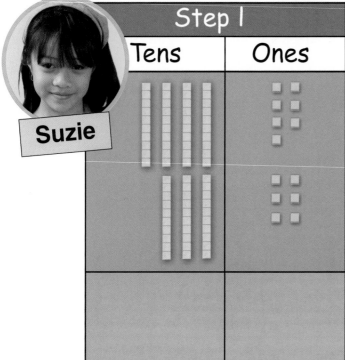

Suzie

Step 1	
Tens	Ones

Step 2	
Tens	Ones

Step 3	
Tens	Ones

Step 4	
Tens	Ones

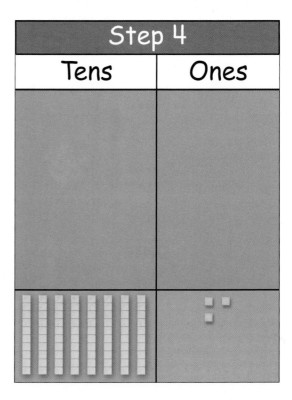

3. How did Billy record Suzie's steps?
   Why didn't he write anything for Suzie's Step 2?
   How did Billy show that **10 ones** were
   traded for **1 ten**?

	Step 1	Step 3	Step 4
Billy	47 +36	¹ 47 +36 3	¹ 47 +36 83

4. How did Rosa record Suzie's steps?
   Why didn't she write anything for Suzie's Step 3?
   Why did she need to write an extra step?

	Step 1	Step 2	Step 4	
Rosa	47 +36	47 +36 13	47 +36 13 +70	47 +36 13 +70 83

5. Use blocks to find the total for each of these.
   Record the steps you used.

A	B	C	D
36 boys 25 girls	16 trucks 27 cars	34 pounds 25 pounds	37 cents 35 cents

1. Pretend that you have 42¢ and you spend 15¢.

   How would you figure out the amount left?

2. How did Kara figure it out?

Kara

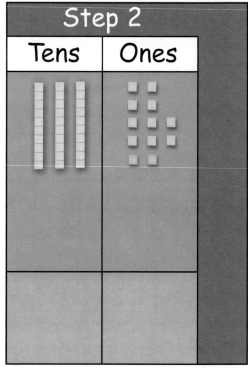

Step 1

Tens	Ones

Step 2

Tens	Ones

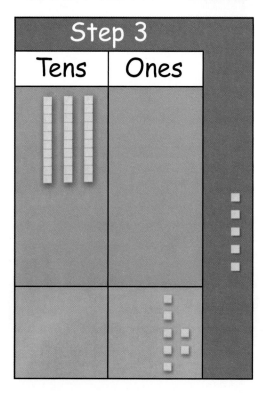

Step 3

Tens	Ones

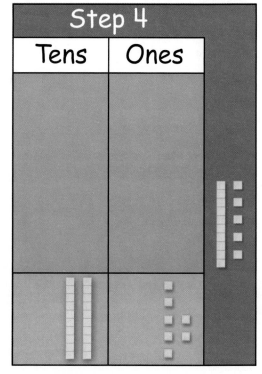

Step 4

Tens	Ones

3. How did Max record Kara's steps?
How did he show that **I ten** was traded for **10 ones**?

	Step I	Step 2	Step 3	Step 4
Max	42 -15	³⁄₁₂ 4̶2̶ -15	³⁄₁₂ 4̶2̶ -15 —— 7	³⁄₁₂ 4̶2̶ -15 —— 27

4. Use blocks to help figure out the amount left for each of the examples below.
Record the steps you used.

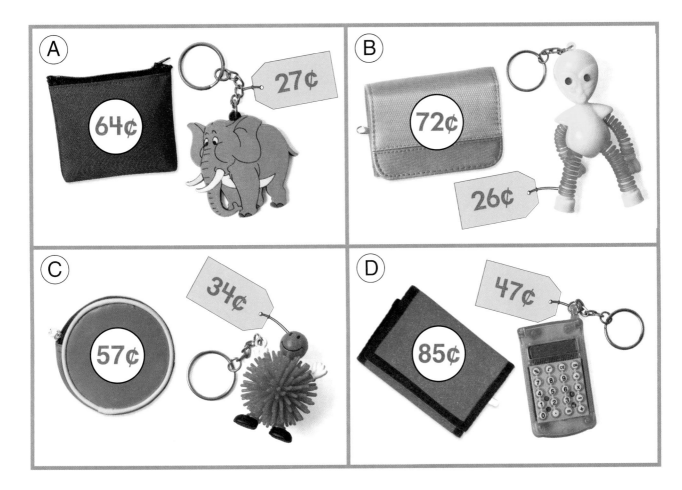

A   64¢   27¢

B   72¢   26¢

C   57¢   34¢

D   85¢   47¢

Pick a ball and a group of dimes and pennies. Which problem makes sense for the things you picked? Solve that problem.

48¢   84¢   51¢

How much money will you have left if you buy the ball?

How much more money do you need to buy the ball?

Tens	Ones
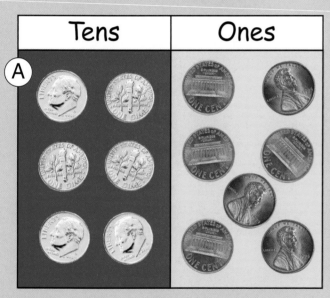
A

Tens	Ones
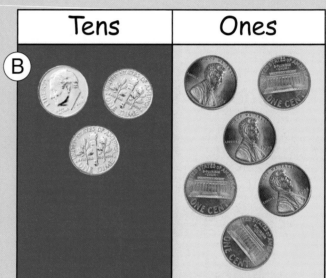
B

Tens	Ones
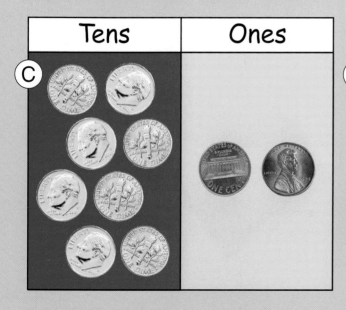
C

Tens	Ones
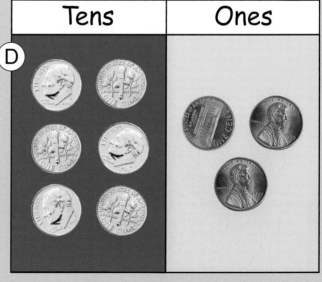
D

Pick a problem about the second-grade art show. Will you add or subtract to solve it? Figure out the answer and show your thinking.

Art Show Visitors		
	Adults	Children
Thursday	39	28
Friday	56	43

A
What was the total number of visitors on Thursday?

B
How many adults in all visited the art show?

C
How many more children visited the art show on Friday than on Thursday?

D
How many more adults than children visited the art show on Thursday?

E
What is the difference between the number of adult visitors on Thursday and Friday?

F
The second-graders made 70 adult tickets for Friday. How many of those tickets were **not** sold?

1. How did each child show **one-half**? How are all 4 pictures of one-half alike? How are they different?

Bianca

Tan

Victor

Shyann

2. What other fraction did each child show? How are those pictures alike? How are they different?

3. Did each child color a greater area for one-half than for one-fourth? Why, or why not?

1. Choose a fraction bug. What shape is it?
   How many **equal parts** does the shape have?

   How many of those equal parts are **red**?

   Write the fraction of the shape that is **red**.

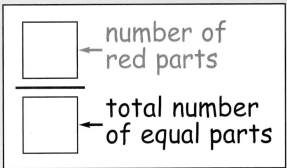

number of red parts ←

total number ← of equal parts

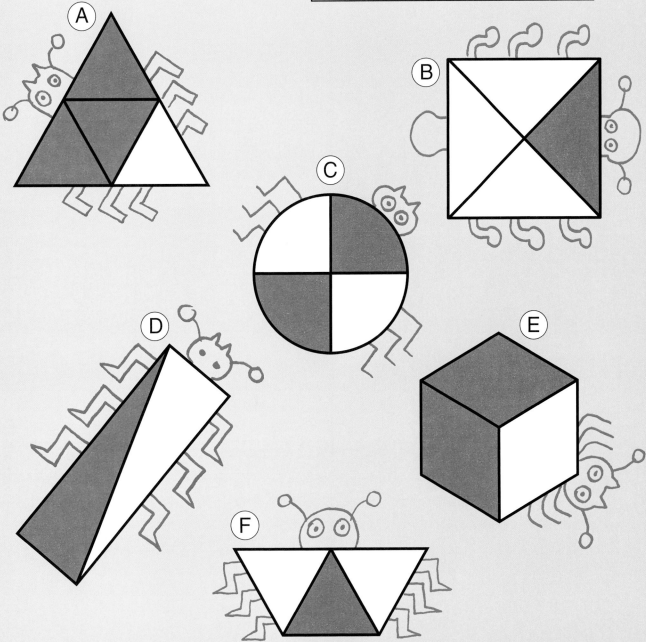

2. Now write the fraction of each shape that is white.

1. Tim and Amy played Fraction Action with these fractions.

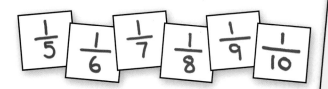

Fraction Action

Toss the cube 6 times. Draw a picture on dot paper to show the fraction you got.

• Which fraction did Amy draw **twice**?

• Which fractions on the cube **didn't** Tim draw?

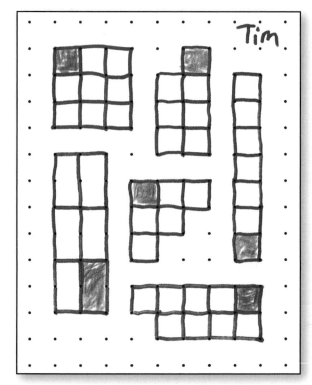

2. Copy this Venn diagram. Write each of the 6 fractions on the correct section of the diagram.

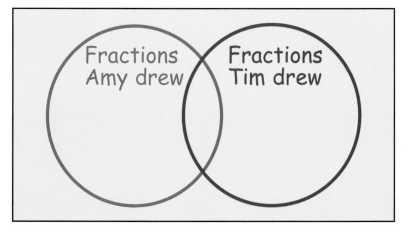

1. Copy and complete this sentence for each array of stamps.

$\frac{1}{2}$ of _____ is _____.

(A)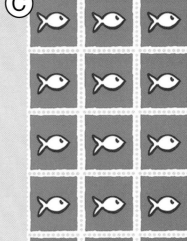

(B)

(C)

(D)

(E)

2. Now copy and complete this sentence for each of the arrays.

$\frac{1}{4}$ of _____ is _____.

3. What do you notice about the two sentences for each array?

1. Ruby used pattern blocks to show some fractions. Then she drew those fractions on dot paper. What fractions of the yellow hexagon did Ruby show?

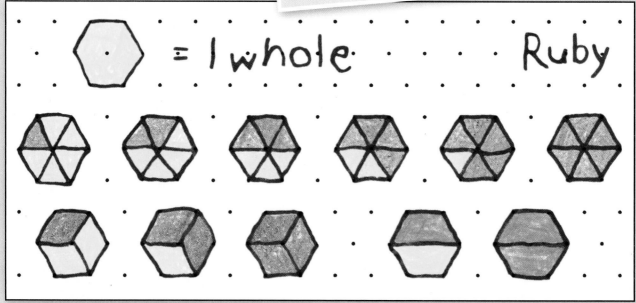

2. Which fraction is greater?
Use Ruby's pictures to help you decide.

$\frac{1}{6}$ or $\frac{3}{6}$ $\frac{1}{3}$ or $\frac{2}{3}$ $\frac{5}{6}$ or $\frac{2}{6}$ $\frac{1}{6}$ or $\frac{1}{3}$ $\frac{1}{2}$ or $\frac{5}{6}$

3. Which of Ruby's fractions are **equivalent** to these?

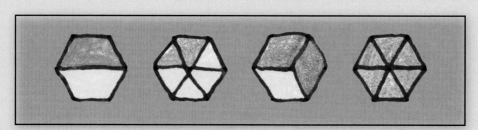

1. Look at each pizza. What fraction can you see? What fraction is missing?

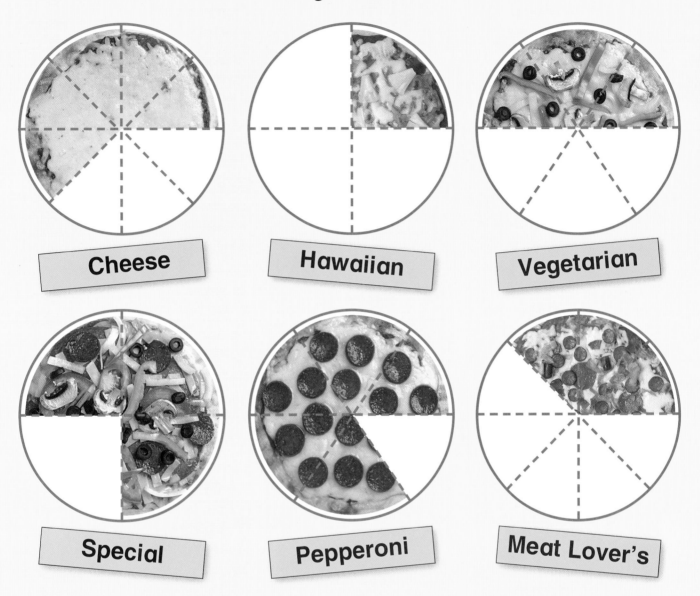

Cheese

Hawaiian

Vegetarian

Special

Pepperoni

Meat Lover's

2. Pick a pizza. Pretend that you eat one piece of it. What fraction of the whole pizza will be left?

3. Answer these questions. Then answer them again for **eighths** and then for **sixths**.

Which 2 pizzas were cut into **fourths**?

If you put all of those **fourths** together, would they make a whole pizza?

1. Which spinner do you think each child used to make his or her tally chart? Explain your thinking.

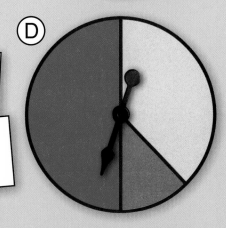

2. Which spinner(s) would you pick to match each of these?

Red is the most likely color.

Red is the least likely color.

Red and blue are equally likely.

Red is less likely than blue.

1. Pick a clock and tell the time.
   Can you say that time a different way?
   What are you usually doing at that time on
   a school-day morning?

Ⓐ 7:15

Ⓑ

Ⓒ

Ⓓ

Ⓔ 8:30

Ⓕ 11:00

Ⓖ

Ⓗ 10:45

2. What time will it be a quarter-hour
   later than each of the times above?

1. At what time did Bear start out on his hike?
   When did he arrive back home?
   What other times do the clocks show?

2. Pick any 2 clocks. What is the difference in time?

Solving Problems Involving Elapsed Time

1. How would you solve Aden's story problem?

2. How did Marie solve the problem?

Aden

I bought 4 packets of basketball cards. There are 6 cards in each packet. How many cards in all did I buy?

Marie

6 + 6 + 6 + 6 = 24

3. Solve these problems. Explain your thinking.

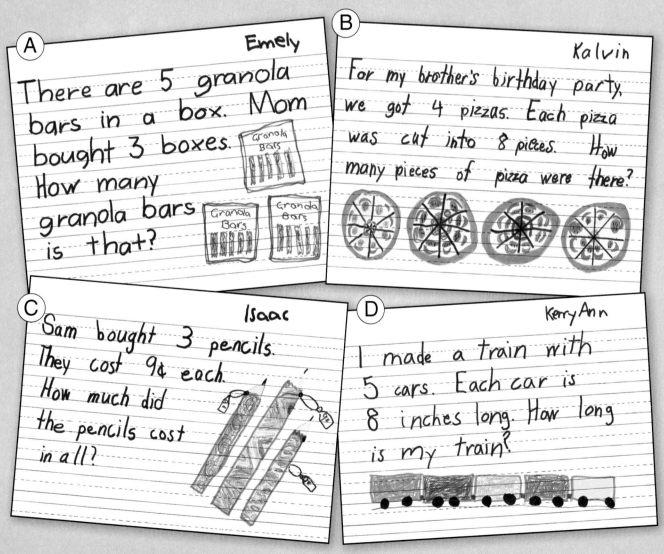

A

Emely

There are 5 granola bars in a box. Mom bought 3 boxes. How many granola bars is that?

Granola Bars

Granola Bars

Granola Bars

B

Kalvin

For my brother's birthday party, we got 4 pizzas. Each pizza was cut into 8 pieces. How many pieces of pizza were there?

C

Isaac

Sam bought 3 pencils. They cost 9¢ each. How much did the pencils cost in all?

D

Kerry Ann

I made a train with 5 cars. Each car is 8 inches long. How long is my train?

Choose one kind of fruit from the juice stand.
How many rows can you see?
How many pieces of fruit are in each row?
Copy and complete the following sentence:

____ rows of ____ is ____ in all.

1. Copy and complete this **multiplication** sentence for each array of stamps.

_____ × _____ = _____

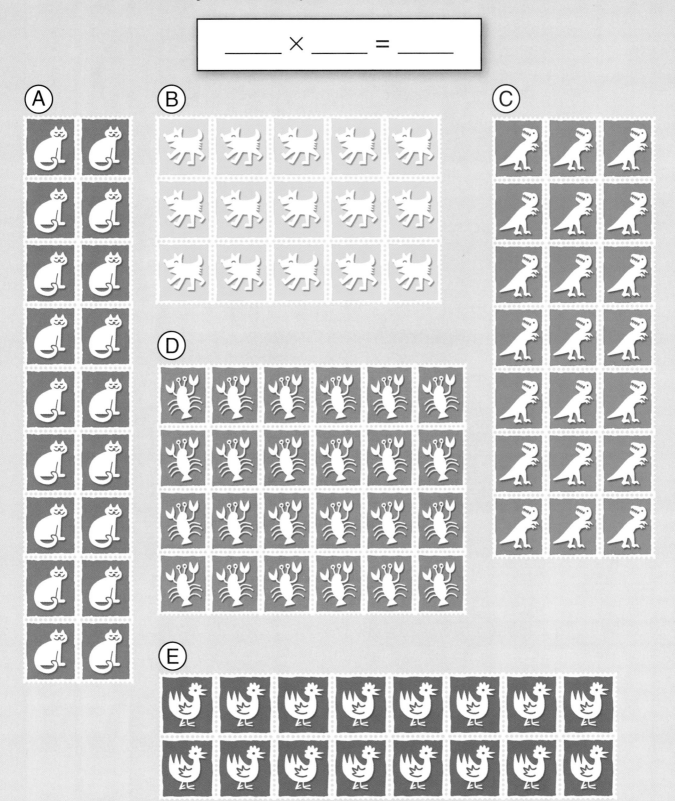

Ⓐ

Ⓑ

Ⓒ

Ⓓ

Ⓔ

2. Now write a multiplication sentence for each kind of fruit on page 82.

1. Write a multiplication sentence for each of these pictures. What do you notice?

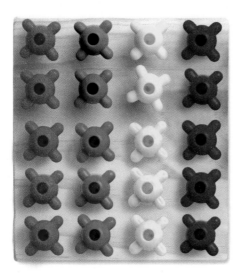 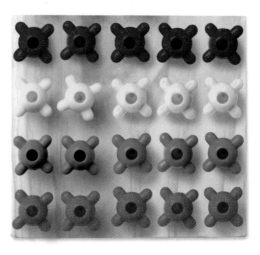

2. Describe each of these arrays in two ways. Write both multiplication sentences.

A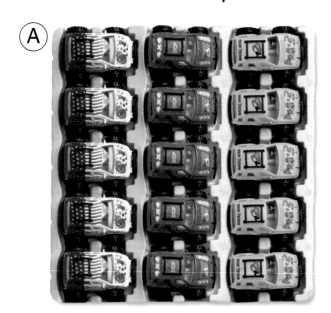

B

C

D

1. How many groups or rows does each picture show? What is a quick way to figure out the total number of things in each picture?

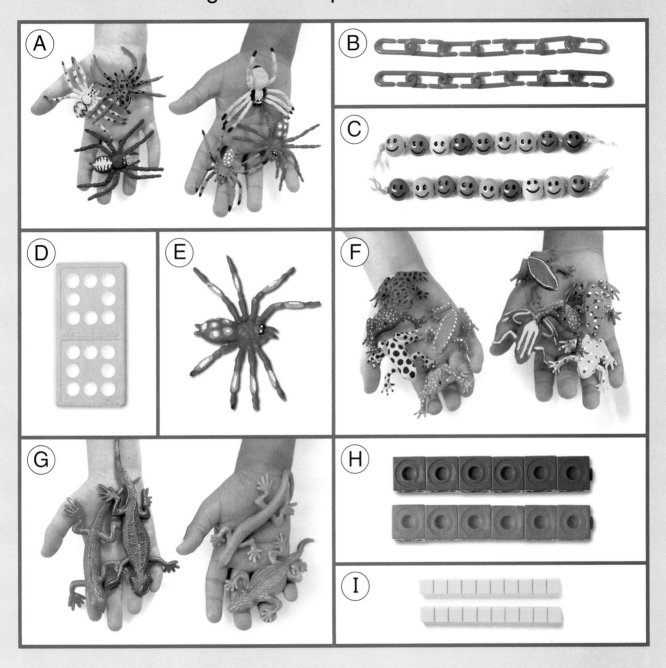

2. Use the pictures to help you complete these "twos" multiplication facts.

2 × 6 = ___	2 × 3 = ___	2 × 9 = ___	2 × 5 = ___
2 × 8 = ___	2 × 10 = ___	2 × 7 = ___	2 × 4 = ___

1. How many groups or rows of **5** does each picture show? What is a quick way to figure out the total number of things in each picture?

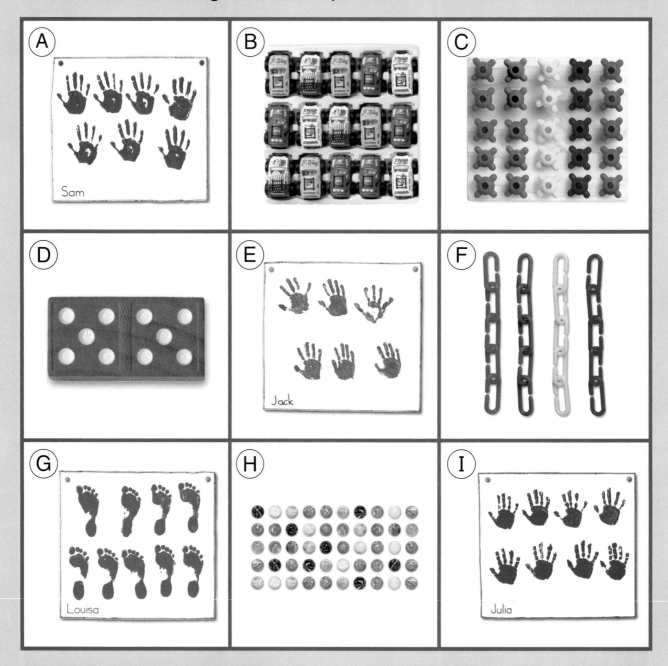

A Sam

B

C

D

E Jack

F

G Louisa

H

I Julia

2. Use the pictures to help you complete these "fives" multiplication facts.

6 × 5 = ___	4 × 5 = ___	7 × 5 = ___	3 × 5 = ___
9 × 5 = ___	8 × 5 = ___	5 × 5 = ___	10 × 5 = ___

Pretend that the monkeys pack **3 bananas** in each box.

1. How many bananas would the monkeys need to fill:

5 boxes? | 7 boxes? | 10 boxes?

2. How many **boxes** in all would the monkeys need for:

12 bananas? | 24 bananas? | 36 bananas?

Now pretend that the monkeys pack **4 bananas** in each box.

3. How many bananas would the monkeys need to fill:

3 boxes? | 5 boxes? | 9 boxes?

4. How many **boxes** in all would the monkeys need for:

16 bananas? | 24 bananas? | 40 bananas?

Pick a coin picture. Pretend that
2 people share the money.
Figure out each person's share.
Copy and complete this sentence:

___¢ divided by 2 is ___¢ each.

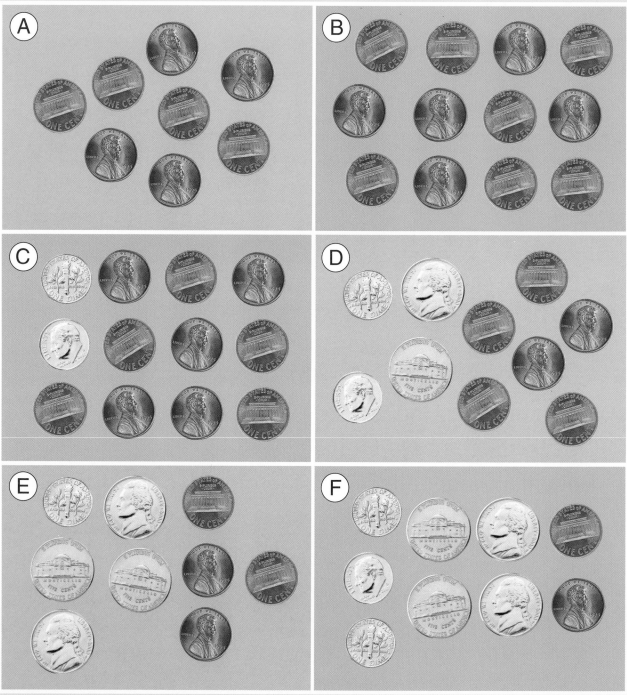

1. Pick an array of stamps and one of these sentences. Copy and complete the sentence.

| ____ divided by 2 is ____ each. |

| ____ divided by 3 is ____ each. |

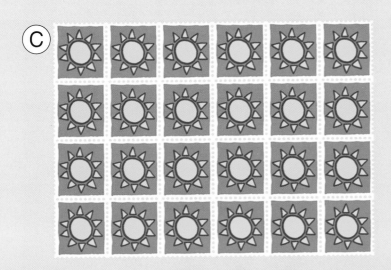

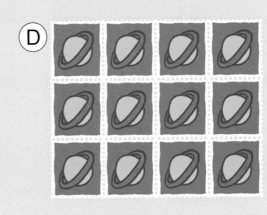

2. Now divide each of these numbers by 4.

20 12 8 24 32

| ____ divided by 4 is ____ each. |

Pick a group of children and a plate of strawberries.

Pretend that the children share the strawberries equally.
How many strawberries will each child get?
Will any strawberries be left over?

Copy and complete this sentence.

____ divided by ____ is ____ each, with ____ left over.

1. Solve each problem. Record your work.

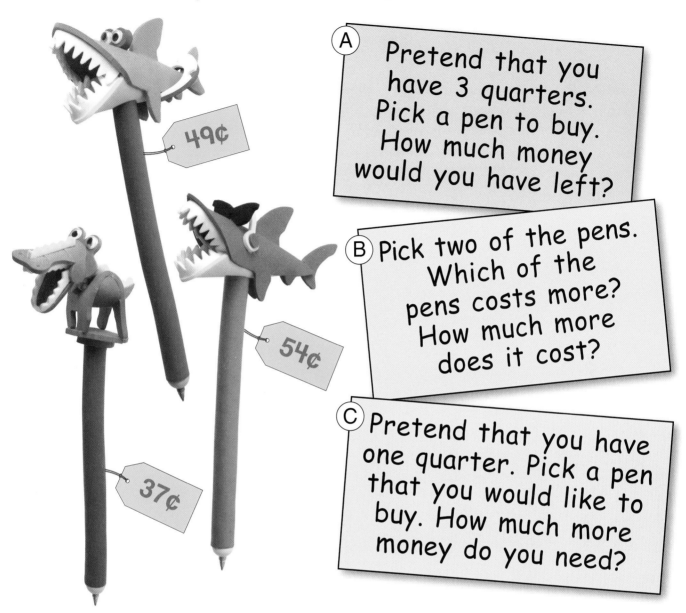

49¢

54¢

37¢

A) Pretend that you have 3 quarters. Pick a pen to buy. How much money would you have left?

B) Pick two of the pens. Which of the pens costs more? How much more does it cost?

C) Pretend that you have one quarter. Pick a pen that you would like to buy. How much more money do you need?

2. Pick a piggy bank and pretend that you have that much money. Then pick a pen and make up a subtraction problem.

82¢   16¢   69¢   38¢

1. Read each problem.
   Will you add or subtract?
   Solve the problem and
   record your work.

$38

$53

$27

$65

$32

$9

A Tahmid bought a basketball shirt and shorts. How much did he spend?

B Kelly bought a basketball hoop. Then she had $16 left. How much money did Kelly have to start with?

C Oscar started with $61 and ended up with $23. What did he buy?

D Rosa has $58. If she buys a basketball, how much will she have left?

E Jed has $25. How much more money does he need to buy the sneakers?

2. Make up and solve some other problems about the things on this page.

1. Rosa figured out the total cost of the children's new bicycles.

Use base-ten blocks to model each of Rosa's steps.

$214

$153

Rosa

Step 1	Step 2	Step 3
214 + 153 — 7	214 + 153 — 67	214 + 153 — 367

2. How else could you find the total cost?

3. Pick any 2 bicycles on this page. Do you think that together they would cost more or less than $500? Figure out the exact cost.

$225

$320

$242

1. How would you figure out the total cost of the Game Station and the game?

$274

Rocket Ride

$60

2. How did these children figure out the total cost?

Rosa

Start at 274. Count by tens.

274   284   294   304   314   324   334

Billy

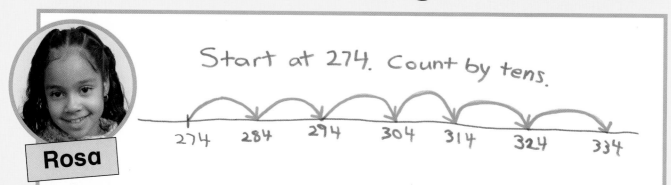

Trade 10 tens.

$$274 + 60 \over 334$$

Kara

Step 1	Step 2	Step 3
$$274 \atop {+\ 60 \over 4}$$	$$\overset{1}{2}74 \atop {+\ 60 \over 34}$$	$$\overset{1}{2}74 \atop {+\ 60 \over 334}$$

3. Add these numbers. Explain your thinking.

266 + 80	326 + 50	283 + 40	457 + 70	382 + 60

1. Pretend that you have $237 and you buy the $50 game. How would you figure out the amount left?

$50

$237

Space Race

2. How did these children figure out the amount left?

Rosa

Start at 237. Count back by tens.

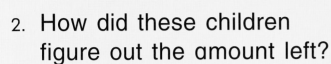

187   197   207   217   227   237

Billy

Trade 1 hundred.

Then take away 5 tens.

$$\begin{array}{r} 237 \\ -\ 50 \\ \hline 187 \end{array}$$

Kara

Step 1	Step 2	Step 3
$$\begin{array}{r} 237 \\ -\ 50 \\ \hline 7 \end{array}$$	$$\begin{array}{r} \overset{1\ \ 13}{2\cancel{3}7} \\ -\ 50 \\ \hline 87 \end{array}$$	$$\begin{array}{r} \overset{1\ \ 13}{2\cancel{3}7} \\ -\ 50 \\ \hline 187 \end{array}$$

3. Subtract these numbers. Explain your thinking.

$$\begin{array}{r} 239 \\ -\ 70 \\ \hline \end{array}$$	$$\begin{array}{r} 466 \\ -\ 80 \\ \hline \end{array}$$	$$\begin{array}{r} 213 \\ -\ 40 \\ \hline \end{array}$$	$$\begin{array}{r} 188 \\ -\ 60 \\ \hline \end{array}$$	$$\begin{array}{r} 107 \\ -\ 40 \\ \hline \end{array}$$

INDEX